Growing Up Is an Adventure, Lord

Growing Up
Is an
Adventure,
Lord

Bible Devotions for Boys

Stephen W. Sorenson

Augsburg
MINNEAPOLIS

GROWING UP IS AN ADVENTURE, LORD
Bible Devotions for Boys

Original text first published as *Lord, Teach Me Your Ways*, © 1988 Abingdon.

Cover design: Eric Lecy
Photos: Robert Cushman Hayes: 18; Jim Whitmer: all other photos including cover.

Library of Congress Cataloging-in-Publication Data

Sorenson, Stephen.
   [Lord, teach me your ways]
   Growing up is an adventure, Lord : Bible devotions for boys /
Stephen W. Sorenson.
       p.   cm.
   Originally published: Lord, teach me your ways. Nashville :
Abingdon, © 1982.
   Summary: A collection of short stories which are modern versions
of Biblical incidents. Each is followed by a brief prayer.
   ISBN 0-8066-2647-X (alk. paper) :
   1. Christian life—Juvenile fiction. 2. Children's stories,
American.   [1. Christian life—Fiction. 2. Short stories.]
I. Title.
[PZ7.S7215Gr   1992]
[Fic]—dc20   92-27056
                                        CIP
                                        AC

The paper used in this publication meets the minimum requirements of American National Standard for Information Sciences—Permanence of Paper for Printed Library Materials, ANSI Z329.48-1984   ∞™

Manufactured in the U.S.A.   AF 9-2647

96   95   94   93   92   1   2   3   4   5   6   7   8   9   10

Dedicated to C. E. S.,
who loves to read
and loves adventures.

Contents

Trapped in Hucky's Cave

Thick, black thunderheads rolled across the sky as David lowered himself into the small cave entrance. "Yuck, it's muddy here. Hope the rest of the cave isn't like this."

John watched David's head disappear into the hole. "I'm not sure I want to go in when the weather's like this. It's after three o'clock, and dinner's at five thirty. Besides, my father told me never to go in here because it isn't safe."

David stuck his head out of the hole. "What difference does the weather make? We'll be inside anyway. Only Tom knows where we are, and our parents think we just went hiking."

"But what about what my father said?"

David chuckled. "My father told me the same thing, but he has never been in this cave. So how does he know? I want to find out what it's like for myself. Are you coming, or not?" He reached up and pulled his old canvas pack toward him.

"I'll come," John said hesitantly, feeling a large raindrop land on his shoulder. *What will happen if I get caught?* he wondered, looking at the nearby cliffs.

"Hey, slowpoke, come on!" David's voice was muffled. John took one last look at the sky and slid down into the muddy ooze. "I'm just in front of you," David said. "Watch your head."

David fished around in the pack until he found the flashlights. They soon discovered that they were in a long passageway about four feet high and six feet wide. Hunched over, they walked past old cans and bottles until the tunnel forked.

"We can't fit in this crack," John said. "We'll have to take the right fork." After they walked by several passageways, he asked, "Are you sure you know how to get back?"

"Sure," David stated confidently. "The other kids come here all the time. See? Look at the arrows on the walls."

The passageway grew larger, and they stood up. Following a few steps behind David, John tried to memorize the passageways. When they reached another fork, David chose the left one.

"How come the red arrows point the other way?" John asked, aiming his light at the wall.

"Somebody was just playing around with spray paint. If you'd quit worrying, you'd have more fun."

After squeezing through a narrow tunnel, they found themselves at the top of a steep ledge. John

10

leaned over the edge. "The footholds aren't deep, and it's about ten feet to the bottom."

"Let's go down," David said impatiently.

Balancing on his stomach, John slid over the edge and put his left foot in the first notch. *Dad told me always to have three parts of my body secure when I climb,* he remembered. Clinging to a rock with both hands, he reached his right foot over to find the next one. He swung to a lower outcropping of rock and climbed the rest of the way down.

"What's it like?" David flashed his light. "It looks easy." He slid over the edge. "I was wondering why you took so long getting down." Hanging onto the rocks, he climbed recklessly down the footholds. Suddenly one of the rocks pulled free, and he tumbled down the last few feet.

"Are you all right?"

"I guess so." David stood up slowly and dusted the damp dirt off his jeans.

"Still want to keep going? Maybe we should do this another time."

"No way." David fingered the dent in his flashlight. "I don't want Tom saying we were scared to go farther."

"But we've gone pretty far already."

"Tom said we'd never get down to the large room, and I want to prove we can." David rubbed his left elbow. "I'm not a quitter. If you're afraid, go back."

"I'll stay," John said, "but let's slow down a little."

David walked past John and started down another passageway. Sometimes they had to crawl through

11

narrow tunnels, and their knees began to hurt. Twice they entered tunnels that didn't have exits, and they had to crawl out backwards. But they didn't have to climb often as they moved through the passageways. The deeper they went, the more they noticed water dripping down the walls and forming muddy pools in low parts of the cave floor.

"Maybe we've gone far enough," John said. "We've been walking nearly an hour."

"No," David countered. "Tom said we'd have to go lower and then higher again."

"How do you know we came the right way? Maybe we're too deep."

"I just know we're going in the right direction." David's voice echoed in the large, musty room.

"I hope you're right." John shook his head. "I lost track of where we are a long time ago."

David pointed toward the muddy ground. "We'll just follow our footprints." He climbed to the top of a six-foot-high bank. "Besides, that room can't be far."

"I've heard you say things like that before," John muttered. "I'm going back in a few minutes." He waited a few seconds and started up the bank.

"I found another room," David called out excitedly.

A moment later, John stood up in the newly discovered room. In one corner, water was streaming into a crack. "Where's all that water coming from? I thought you said this cave stays pretty dry."

"That's what Tom told me."

"Did he ever come in here when it was raining?" John walked over to the water.

David shrugged his shoulders. "Who cares? The water is going below us anyway."

"I'm going back. I don't like this cave."

"But we haven't found the room yet! Are you scared?"

"My father says it's OK to be scared sometimes," John said firmly. "He says . . . ."

"I don't care," David interrupted. "You're just a scaredy-cat."

"Maybe I am." John's voice quivered. "I've never gone caving before, and I'm not sure I like it."

"All right, we'll turn back in a few minutes." David gave John a dirty look.

After resting for ten minutes in the large room, John began to climb down the six-foot-high bank and stopped suddenly. "I hear water dripping."

David shone his light down. "Look, water is coming into the room, and that hollow is half full already! What will we do now?"

"We'll just have to wait for the water to go down." John scrambled back up.

"That could take days. What if it keeps rising?" David clenched his fists. "I can't even swim."

"Don't ask me," John snapped. "You were the one who was so eager to come down here."

"You had a choice, too." David looked down at the water again.

"Yeah," John said slowly. "I knew I shouldn't have come. My father knows what he's talking about."

"I came mostly because of Tom," David replied. "He dared me to do it."

"Who cares what he thinks?" John said. "Sometimes a dare is dumb. Let's turn off the flashlights to save the batteries."

Sitting in the darkness, they couldn't even see their hands, but they could hear the water running below them. "Maybe it is good to be afraid of some things," David said.

"If I had listened to my father, I wouldn't have given in," John replied.

The time passed slowly, and the boys quit talking. Their fears grew.

"Look," David said suddenly. "There's a light!"

"We're in here," John shouted.

Someone sloshed through the water several minutes later, and a beam of light blinded them. "Come down, boys. I'm Norm Peterson, and I'm here to get you out. You'll get wet anyway, and the water will get even deeper." The man's husky voice was kind.

"But I can't swim," David said.

"You'll make it. The water isn't that deep yet. It's a good thing you didn't go down any lower."

"How'd you find us?" John asked, sliding down the bank.

"Your friend Tom told his mother that you were in the cave. When you didn't show up for dinner, someone called her to see if she knew where you were. Then the police called me because I know every inch of this cave. In three hours, this room will be full of water." Mr. Peterson began to lead them through a twisting passageway. "Walk slowly, and hold hands," he cautioned. "This shortcut will take us through lots of water."

John's wet pants clung to his knees; his teeth began to chatter. "Are we almost there?"

"It's not too far." Mr. Peterson picked his way along the slippery rocks. John and David trailed behind. "Watch yourselves here. The water is running down several tunnels. Fall in one and you'll drown." Before the boys had a chance to think, the man led them into another room full of waist-high water. The mud sucked at their shoes, and John almost lost his balance.

"Once we go around a pit, we're out," Mr. Peterson said, helping them climb up a steep bank. "There's a small path just to the left of the pit. Keep your eyes straight ahead and crawl slowly. He pointed to John. "You go first." He took a rope out of his nylon knapsack and tied one end around John's waist.

His left shoulder brushing the rock wall, John crawled past the pit and up the damp clay to the other side. "That's far enough," Mr. Peterson said. "Untie the rope." He turned to David. "Now it's your turn," he said as he tied the rope around David's waist. "Don't look in the pit."

David began crawling. Halfway across, he glanced down and froze. "I can't move," he said, his voice rising. "My legs won't move."

"You can do it," the man reassured him. "Just move your right knee ahead five inches. Good. Now the left one." Inch by inch, David crawled along the narrow path. When he reached John, he knocked a rock loose. It rolled over the edge and bounced for a long time, and then the boys heard a splash.

Mr. Peterson coiled the rope and crawled to the boys. David lay on his back, staring blankly toward the ceiling and breathing heavily. "Are we almost out?" John asked again.

"Yes," Mr. Peterson answered. When John saw a circle of light a few moments later, he quickened his pace. Closely followed by David, he climbed out of the cave.

"Oh, John, thank God you're all right," his mother said.

His father gave him a long hug. "It's good to see you. Uncle Frank nearly drowned in there when we were kids. Whole sections of the cave fill up with water." John couldn't look his father in the eye. "You owe a lot to Mr. Peterson," his father continued. "If he hadn't been willing to go after you, you'd still be in there."

"I know," John said thoughtfully as he and his parents stood on the muddy hill.

LET'S THINK ABOUT IT

Because they chose to disobey their fathers' warnings, John and David nearly drowned in Hucky's Cave. As the Israelites traveled through the wilderness, they ran out of water at a place called Rephidim and threatened to kill Moses unless he found them something to drink. Moses prayed, and God told him to strike a certain rock with his staff. Moses obeyed, and enough water gushed out of the rock to satisfy the Israelites' needs. When a similar situation happened again, God told Moses to speak to another rock rather than striking it, but Moses disobeyed. You can read about these incidents, and how God punished Moses for his disobedience, in the Old Testament—Exodus 17:1-7; Numbers 20:2-13.

◆　　◆　　◆

Lord, I know it's important for me to obey my parents, but sometimes I want to make my own decisions anyway. Sometimes I want to prove to my friends that I'm not afraid to do things that I shouldn't be doing. Help me refuse to do something wrong just because someone dares me to do it and teach me how to stand up for what's right even when my friends try to change my mind. Amen.

Adventure on the Old Logging Road

"I'm sure glad we live so close to the national forest," Jenny said, following her brother down the rocky path.

Roger ducked under a low branch. "Yeah. It's nice to be able to walk out the back door and follow these trails. Do you think we'll see a deer again?"

"Maybe," Jenny said, pushing her hair off her neck. "We saw one about this time a few weeks ago."

When they came to a fork, Roger paused. "Let's take the old logging road. We haven't gone that way for a long time."

They followed a stream until they reached a clearing. "Look at the tire tracks!" Jenny exclaimed. "I didn't know that people could still drive back here."

"Let's see where they go."

Without realizing it, they walked up to the side of a large truck almost surrounded by bushes in a grove of trees. "It's covered with camouflage netting," Roger said, "the kind they have in the army surplus store."

Jenny walked around to the back of the truck. "I wonder what it's doing here?" she asked. "Maybe somebody stole it."

"Don't be dumb," Roger said. "It's probably just a park service truck."

"No it isn't," Jenny said, "and I'm not dumb. Park service trucks don't have to be hidden."

As Roger began to answer, they heard an engine. "We'd better hide," Roger said, "just in case."

"I told you it might be stolen," Jenny stated as they scrambled into a nearby clump of bushes.

A panel truck moved slowly into the clearing and backed up next to the large truck. Two men in their twenties got out. "Things sure went easy today, Phillip," one of them said, grinning. "It's not a bad way to end the week. We've hit every town in the area."

"We're not through yet, Mark," Phillip replied, opening the back door of the panel truck. "We still have to get all the bikes to Kansas."

"They'll pay a pretty penny for this load," Mark said, pulling out a shiny ten-speed. "This one must have cost nearly three hundred dollars."

"Yeah, and the owner only put on that tiny lock that even a baby could have taken off. Our bolt cutters cut through it like butter."

Roger elbowed Jenny in the ribs. "Those guys are stealing bikes," he whispered. "Maybe they're the ones who took Kevin's bike."

20

"Shh," Jenny said. "I want to hear what they're saying."

"Do you think Old Man Rogers will get the new water pump in this truck by midnight?" Mark asked, removing the camouflage netting. "I want to get out of here."

"Don't worry. He gets paid enough to do the work and keep his mouth shut."

"But he told me last night that he's getting edgy."

"This is our last day here for a good while," Phillip said, "so he shouldn't worry. He'll get the repairs done tonight because he has to, and we'll leave on schedule. That's part of our deal." He handed a motor scooter to Mark, who had climbed into the truck. "These little gas savers are going to fetch a good price too."

Hardly daring to breathe, Roger and Jenny remained motionless. The men quit talking and furiously loaded the large truck. Then they started both trucks and drove away.

As soon as the sound of engines died away, Jenny and Roger stood up and started running. "What'll we do?" Roger asked, catching his breath when they reached the creek. "We can't just let them get away. But they may have guns." He paused. "I don't want to see them again. That one guy was especially mean looking."

"And Mr. Rogers has dogs," Jenny said, "the kind like the junkyard has." She shuddered, thinking of the huge dog that jumped up on the fence while her father was getting a new snowtire rim for the car.

21

"Let's tell Mom and Dad," Roger suggested. "They'll know what to do. We're not the right people to get involved in this."

"But what if the truck isn't really in the garage? Then we'd look foolish and people would think we just made the whole thing up." Jenny picked up a stone and threw it into a small pool. "No, we'll have to make sure it's inside before we tell anyone about it, and we have to do that ourselves."

Roger looked up at the sky. "It'll be dark before too long, and there will be a full moon tonight. We won't be able to sneak up on them."

"We have to try, anyway. Rogers' Garage is the only place in town big enough to hold their truck, and it's way past the school."

"We could take the shortcut behind the school," Roger added, and off they went. They stopped at their house long enough to remove a flashlight from a hook in the shed and then hurried toward the school.

"What if the dogs are outside?" Jenny asked suddenly, her soft voice sounding loud in the evening stillness. "They're trained to attack people. And maybe somebody is outside, keeping a lookout. We haven't even told Mom and Dad!"

"Too late to worry about that now," Roger said. "We're almost there." They crossed the road near the school and cut through the ravine behind the meadow. "There's the chain link fence he put around all his old cars," Roger said. "We'll stay in the shadows and crawl around back until we can peep in a window."

Jenny got down on her hands and knees and began crawling. "There's glass on the ground," she whispered. "Be careful." Not far from the garage, she brushed against a tin can, and it rolled into the fence.

"Who's there?" a man's loud voice suddenly called out. "Who is it?"

Jenny felt her heart pounding; Roger flattened himself on the ground.

"Come out," the man said again.

"You're just nervous," another man said. "It's just one of those cats."

"Maybe so," the first man said, shining his flashlight along the fence. "But I want to be sure." When the beam of light hit Jenny's back, she felt like jumping up and running away, but she froze and the light passed her by.

"Let's go in and get another cup of coffee," the second man said. "Old Man Rogers is coming along well with the truck, and he'll be taking a break soon to let the dogs out. They'll smell anyone who is around."

Jenny stiffened. *Oh, no,* she thought. *We'll get caught for sure. We won't even get to look in the window. What'll we do now?*

"Get going," her brother whispered as the garage door clanged shut. "We have to look inside. We're the only ones who can do it. If we wait, they'll leave before anyone can catch them.

They continued crawling, and Jenny wished that she hadn't worn her good jacket. The dead grass next to the fence crunched; a car horn echoed in the distance.

Jenny slowly eased her way up to the window and looked inside. The two men they had seen earlier were drinking coffee, and Mr. Rogers was talking to them. "The truck is in there," she whispered, ducking down, "but I can't see any bicycles."

"They're probably inside the truck," Roger said. "Let's get out of here before he lets the dogs out. I bet if they smell us they can jump right over this fence."

They crawled back and started running as soon as they reached the street. "Hurry up," Jenny called over her shoulder. "We have to tell Mom and Dad what we've seen."

Both of them burst into the kitchen where their father was setting the table. "Dad," Jenny said, "we've found some bike thieves and a truck that's in Mr. Rogers' Garage. And they're leaving tonight if we don't stop them!"

"Hold on a minute," Mr. Jamison said. "What's this about bike thieves, and who is leaving, and why are you getting home so late?"

Roger and Jenny took turns explaining what they had seen. The more they explained, the more serious their father's expression became. "Don't you know," he finally said, "that you shouldn't get involved in something like that by yourselves? They could have hurt you." Then his eyes softened and he smiled. "But I'd have done the same thing if I were you, even though it was a scary thing to do. I'll call the police and let them handle things."

As he was dialing, Jenny turned to Roger. "I'm glad we didn't chicken out," she said, "even though

I didn't think we could get close enough to see the truck. Now maybe Kevin will get his bike back." She sat down in a chair. "You know, we finally had a real adventure."

Roger grinned. "It's about time."

LET'S THINK ABOUT IT

Gideon, like Jenny and Roger, at first wasn't sure he wanted to become involved in something dangerous. When God told Gideon that he would go to battle against the Midianites, Israel's enemies, Gideon came up with all sorts of excuses and tests, which are found in the Old Testament—Judges 6:11-22, 36-40. But after Gideon finally decided to trust God, he led a surprise attack on the Midianites, using trumpets, empty jars, and torches instead of weapons! You can read about the attack in Judges 7:19-23.

◆   ◆   ◆

Thank you, God, for creating me with a sense of adventure. Please help me explore my opportunities and use them to become the person you created me to be. Increase my faith in you and help me be faithful in even the smallest tasks. Amen.

Sabotage at Crystal Park Raceway

"Look at your brother go!" Mr. Timms exclaimed. "He found the lines on that curve perfectly."

Timothy watched his brother's minibike disappear over a hill in a cloud of dust, followed closely by three other racers. "Justin still has three laps to go, Dad. Anything can happen."

"But he can do it. It would mean so much to him if he wins today. He'll be able to attend the awards banquet honoring the best amateur riders in the district."

Timothy walked closer to the thirty-foot-wide track. More than twenty minibikes whined past him, vying for position. Minutes later, Justin rode by again, adjusting his body carefully to maintain balance on the treacherous series of small bumps that lay just before the curve. His minibike spun around the curve, spitting sand.

"Did you see Justin gas it past those other two riders and cut into the curve again?" Mr. Timms said excitedly. "He's right up front. If he keeps up that pace, he'll be in good shape for the second heat."

"Yeah, I saw it," Timothy answered. "He looked reckless to me."

"He's a good rider," Mr. Timms said, "and he knows a lot about racing. Why, he has only been racing a year, and if he wins this race he'll have enough points to move from Amateur to Expert class."

And I'm still a novice, Timothy thought, wishing his younger brother hadn't started riding. *Mom and Dad used to be proud of me, and now they talk about how good Justin is.* He looked down at his smooth-soled work boots. *I have to ride a used minibike while Justin gets a new one.*

"Let's hurry over to the finish line," Mrs. Timms said as the dust began to settle. "I want to be there when Justin comes in."

They walked across the track's infield and stopped about 150 feet from the finish line. A rider dressed in orange flashed by, and the referee hung up the white flag. "Just one more lap," Mr. Timms shouted. As Justin and another rider passed them, he yelled, "Flat out, Justin. Go for it!"

Waiting anxiously, Mr. and Mrs. Timms watched the top of the last hill for Justin's yellow and white outfit. Timothy sat down on a rock, looking as if he didn't really care.

"He's doing it, Timothy," Mrs. Timms said. "Look, he just overtook that other boy in the valley." The engine screaming, Justin's minibike crossed the finish line four feet in front of his closest pursuer.

"Wasn't that a great final lap?" Mr. Timms turned to Timothy. "You sure don't seem very excited about your brother's win. If he wins the second heat, he'll be one of the top racers."

Timothy forced a smile. "Yeah."

"Well, I did it," Justin said as they walked over to their pickup truck. "Now if I can only do that again, I'll have enough points to win the race." He turned to Timothy. "How'd you do in your first heat?"

"I came in tenth," Timothy said slowly.

"Keep practicing and it'll come," Justin stated. "Just wait until I get home and tell Roger and James. They won't believe it."

I hope they don't, Timothy thought. *You have all the luck.*

"I'm going to watch the last part of the Experts race," Justin said to his parents as he refilled the gas tank. "Want to come with me? Doug Walker is really coming up in the standings, and he says that he'll give me some tips as soon as I move into the Expert Class."

"When did he say that?" Mrs. Timms asked.

"Just before my first heat started," Justin answered.

"Are you coming too?" Mr. Timms looked at Timothy. "You could probably learn something."

"I have to check a few things on my bike, Dad. My second heat starts pretty soon."

"OK. We'll try to be there when your race starts."

Timothy put on his leather jacket and cleaned his goggles. *Justin wins again,* he thought, *and I'm still way back in the pack.* He picked up Justin's yellow jacket and then dropped it. *Justin gets all the nice stuff. I'm still wearing the first jacket Mom bought me.*

As he hopped on his 80cc minibike, he looked once more at his brother's shiny new one. Suddenly he leaned down, pulled the fuel line hose on Justin's minibike off the carburetor, and let the gasoline squirt onto the ground. *That should be about right,* he thought, carefully replacing the hose on the carburetor. He then walked over to a steep hill and watched the older boys and girls roar past him on larger motorcycles.

About forty-five minutes later, the loudspeakers blared out that the Novice class would soon be starting its second heat. Timothy walked back to the pickup, hoping that his father would be there to help him with last-minute details. But he wasn't. *They don't really care that much about me,* he thought. *They're too busy trying to teach Justin new techniques so that he'll keep winning races. It's as if I weren't even racing today.* He kicked a small cactus plant, and it broke off at the base.

He pushed his minibike up to the line just in front of the gate. The official walked by, making sure all the minibikes were the same distance from the gate and then held up the two-minute sign. Timothy's minibike started on the second kick, and the engines roared as the boys and girls warmed up their minibikes. Then the official held up the one-minute sign.

Timothy positioned his goggles and made sure that his fuel switch was on. After the racers in the lineup indicated they were ready to start, the official put the one-minute sign sideways, and another man dropped the gate.

Timothy fought for a place in the tightly bunched group, maneuvering for the lines he had picked on the first curve. He skidded around the curve, neck and neck with several other riders, and when the trail narrowed, he was one of the leaders! He shifted gears smoothly and opened up the throttle. The minibike shot up the hill and over a jump. He hit hard and shifted down to go over the smaller bumps that could spin his minibike sideways in an instant. Squinting into the sun, he put his foot down hard on the next curve, cutting sharply to the inside.

With only two laps to go, Timothy was in fifth place. As he rounded the curve near the finish line, his father shouted, "Come on, Timothy. Don't hold it back. Open her up!"

Timothy gritted his teeth. *I'm doing the best I can. Why does he expect me to do as well as Justin?*

When Timothy passed the finish line again, he saw the white flag and knew that he had to make his move. He shot up the hill, over the jump, and landed in soft dirt. The minibike skidded sideways, but he regained control. By suddenly cutting inside, he passed two more riders on the worst curve on the track. Two riders ahead of him were trying to out-maneuver one another, and leaning forward, he shot up behind them on the straightaway. He hardly

31

slowed down as he entered the next to the last turn. His foot stretched out for control, and he passed both riders.

"You've got it!" Mr. Timms yelled, but Timothy couldn't hear his words over the noise of the engines and the spectators.

"Nice going, Timothy." His dad clapped him on the back as he wheeled the minibike back to the truck. "You sure rode well."

"Thanks. It's hard to believe I really won." Suddenly Timothy remembered his brother. "Dad, has the Amateur race started yet?"

"It just started. We may still have time to watch Justin if we hurry and get this stuff in the pickup. Mom is by the second curve."

Timothy parked his minibike and walked over to the track. The riders were on their first lap, and Justin was third. "He's still doing well," Mr. Timms said, "and he might earn enough points from the race today to be invited to the banquet. He has improved so much during the past six months."

"What about me?" Timothy asked. "I'm getting better, too."

"Of course you are," Mr. Timms said. "I never said you weren't. It's just that your brother isn't good in other sports like you are because he's so small for his age. Your mother and I try to encourage him as much as we can."

"Is that why you bought him a new minibike and didn't buy me one?"

Mr. Timms turned and looked at Timothy. "Is that how you feel? Why didn't you tell me? Your mother and I planned to give you something this Christmas, but I guess it wouldn't hurt to tell you now. We bought you a motorcycle. You are getting too big for that minibike, and soon you'll have to move into motorcycle racing."

Timothy swallowed hard. "You mean, you bought a new one for me and didn't tell me?" he finally asked.

"That's right."

Timothy looked out onto the track. "But I haven't been winning as much as Justin has."

"Winning isn't the only important thing," his father said. "You try hard, and you have fun. I don't believe that somebody your age should be forced to compete so hard in any activity that when he loses he becomes upset."

"Like what Mr. Leonardi does to Craig in Little League?" Timothy said. "If Craig misses a catch or strikes out, his father really yells at him."

"That's exactly what I mean. I think you're doing your best, and that's what counts. Besides, you're learning important lessons, both when you race and when you help me maintain the minibike."

Timothy watched the track carefully, feeling upset. *And I was jealous just because Justin could do something better than I could.*

Justin came flying over a jump and then his engine began to miss. A few seconds later, it stopped running altogether. "What's wrong?" Mr. Timms shouted from the other side of the track.

"I don't know. It quit running. It just quit running." Tears welled up in Justin's eyes. "And I was in second place, too."

As soon as the other contestants passed him, Justin pushed the minibike across the track and up to the pickup truck. "It was running really well, and then it quit."

Mr. Timms unscrewed the top on the gas tank and looked inside. "That's your problem. It's empty."

"But I filled it up again this morning. It should have had plenty of gasoline."

"That certainly is strange."

Timothy felt like a weight was sitting on his chest. "Justin, I have something to tell you, and. . . ."

"Go on, Timothy," his father said.

"I can't tell you how rotten I feel," Timothy said as he finished telling what he had done. "It's just that you keep winning, and I felt jealous. Can you forgive me?"

Justin thought for a moment. "Yeah, I've been jealous of you plenty of times, too, especially when you got on the football team. But I sure feel bad about not finishing the race." He looked up at his father. "You always say that winning isn't the most important thing, though."

Mr. Timms smiled. "Sons, I'm proud of both of you."

"So am I," Mrs. Timms said.

The gate dropped, and another group of boys and girls began racing.

LET'S THINK ABOUT IT

When Timothy became jealous of his brother, he didn't understand the whole picture. He didn't realize that his parents were being fair to him, too, so he needlessly ruined his brother's chances to win the race. In the Old Testament—Genesis 37:1-36—you can read how Joseph's brothers became so jealous of him that they threw him into a pit and sold him as a slave! Later, in Genesis 45, after God helped Joseph become a high Egyptian official, he met his brothers and forgave them.

◆　　◆　　◆

I don't like it when my brother or sister receives more than I do, Lord. It's hard for me to be happy sometimes unless I'm the one who is getting something new. Please take away the jealousy I feel and give me more love. Thank you that you forgive me as I forgive others. Amen.

Who Is My Neighbor?

"We've learned what it means to love our neighbor as ourselves," Mr. Shaver said, "but who is our neighbor? This point is the key to what we've been talking about this morning."

"The people in my apartment building," Paul replied, looking down at his Sunday school lesson.

"Everybody in trouble," Greg stated, watching the boys in the next room stack their chairs against the wall.

"We should really care about everyone, not just be nice to people because we're supposed to," Brad said.

"Well," Mr. Shaver said, turning around in his chair, "according to my watch it's time to quit, and you guys have to hurry over to Brad's house to catch a ride to the park. Stack your chairs, and don't forget to pick up the Sunday school papers by the door."

The five boys quickly stacked the chairs and walked out the side door by the choir room. "That was some class," Tyrone said as he opened the door at the top of the stairs and stepped outside. "I've heard that a thousand times. Everybody knows that stuff."

"I didn't learn anything new, either," Brad chimed in. He loosened the top button of his shirt. "Whew, it's hot. I hope they have lots of lemonade at the picnic."

"We'd better hurry," Tyrone said. "We'll have to pack the car, and if we're too late we may not be able to use the baseball diamond."

"And we'll have to change clothes too," Brad said. "My mother wouldn't let me wear jeans this morning like I wanted to."

As the boys cut across the church parking lot, they heard a crash. "Look!" Eric exclaimed. "Somebody flipped over on his bicycle."

"So what?" Tyrone said. "We're late already."

"But he's getting up so slowly."

"He's probably just taking his time," Brad said, turning to Tyrone. Noticing that Greg and Eric had stopped, he turned around. "Hey, aren't you guys coming?"

"We'll come in a minute."

Lee, a stocky, curly-haired boy, squinted into the sun. "That's Randy Williams. He plays with his little sister in the park every day after school. I don't want to have anything to do with that sissy." He followed Brad and Tyrone.

Eric and Greg ran over to Randy. "Are you OK?" Eric asked.

"I guess so." Randy was holding his hand against his forehead, and Eric noticed a trickle of blood.

"Why don't you go to the church office, Greg, and get some gauze pads and adhesive tape? I'll take him to the washroom in Fellowship Hall to wash out the cut. We'll meet you there."

"At first my head was numb," Randy said, "but now it's starting to hurt."

"We'll get you fixed up," Eric reassured. "It's not as deep as it looks. Cuts on the head always bleed a lot."

Randy noticed the large rip in his pants. "It happened so fast. I was hurrying to get home from the store and that towel in my basket caught in the spokes. I saw you guys standing there as I went by, and then I was on the sidewalk."

"We heard you fall."

"Where'd the other boys go?"

"We're all going to a church picnic," Eric said, picking up the groceries. "Hey, your milk isn't leaking."

"That's good." Randy looked at the torn grocery bag. "My name's Randy. What's yours?"

"Eric."

"What were you guys doing by the church?"

"We go to that church."

Randy looked up at the tall steeple and then at the cars in the parking lot. "My family used to go to church, but we quit going when Dad got sick and Mom went to work. Thanks for helping me."

"That's OK. I'm glad we were here." Eric removed the towel from the spokes and stacked the groceries in the baskets. "If you feel better, maybe you would like to go with us to Plum Lake. I could tell Mom to bring more hamburger."

"Thanks," Randy said, "but I have to get this food home and by then it'd be too late."

"I could call my friends and tell them to leave without us," Eric said, "and my father could drive us over."

"I'll ask my mother," Randy said, a smile creeping across his face. "I think she'll let me go."

LET'S THINK ABOUT IT

An expert in Old Testament law tried to trap Jesus by asking him difficult questions. Jesus told the expert a story similar to the story you just read and answered the question, "Who is my neighbor?" The story is found in the New Testament—Luke 10:25-37.

◆　◆　◆

Lord, When I see someone who needs help, make me willing to do what I can to help. I don't always want to be bothered, especially if the person isn't very popular. You want me to be kind to everyone, just as I'd want people to be kind to me. Amen.

Mrs. Penner's Surprise

"He missed the ball!" a tall boy on the sidelines said, shaking his head. "It popped up right to him, and he missed it."

The other boys watched Paul run after the ball while the winning runner passed second base. Finally, Paul stopped the ball and threw it as hard as he could toward home plate. It bounced feebly near second base, however, and before anyone could pick up the ball again the runner scored.

"That's it," the coach called out.

Bunched together in small groups, the boys headed into the gym for the assembly.

Paul waited a minute before going in. *Why can't I catch those?* He took off his thick glasses and then put them back on. *The eye doctor said I'd be able to judge distances with these new lenses.*

He walked into the gym and sat in the second row of bleachers. "What happened?" a boy asked him. "Tony and Rick sure were angry when you dropped that ball."

"I don't know, Jared," Paul answered. "I just lost it."

"That's easy to do," Jared agreed. "I wonder how long this assembly will take?"

"Not long," Paul said. "It's the final details about the auction."

"What are you going to bring?" Jared asked. "My mother decided to donate our gas dryer. She wants an electric one and figures this is as good a time as any to buy a new one."

Paul shook his head. "I don't know. Mom and I really don't have anything valuable to give away, even though we want to help."

The principal walked up to the microphone. "Boys and girls, we have received word that the family from Cambodia we're sponsoring will arrive next week. You all know about the auction tomorrow and how we have invited the whole city to come and bid. You also know that the class that raises the most money will win a field trip to Starved Rock State Park. Now we need to let you know that a crew of volunteers will be at the gym from eight to eleven tomorrow morning to help you and your parents drop off your donations."

"I'm bringing a ten-speed bicycle that my brother doesn't want anymore," a girl behind Paul whispered. "It should be worth at least fifty dollars."

After a few more announcements, the assembly was over. Paul pulled the books out of his locker and walked back down the stairs. "Hey, Frog-eyes," Tony said loudly, cutting across the hall. "That was some play you made today." He looked Paul in the eye. "What are you bringing to the auction to help our class win?"

"I don't know yet."

Tony laughed forcefully. "You don't? You've had a whole week to line something up. Why," he continued, "my father is donating a scope from his hunting rifle."

Paul walked out the door alone, thinking hard. Out of habit, he kicked an empty pop can, and then he had an idea. *There are a lot of cans in the park barrels and along the roads. I could pick up whole bags of them, sell them in the grocery store, and use the money for the auction.*

Unlocking his front door, he laid down his knapsack on the faded couch. *Since there isn't a note on the table,* he thought, *I guess Mom will be home from work at the usual time.* He walked into the small kitchen, poured himself a glass of water, and then rounded up two old pillowcases. After changing clothes, he brought his old wagon from the basement and wrote a note to let his mother know he'd be home late.

Ten minutes later, he started picking up cans along Lee Highway and worked his way toward the park. Even though Robin Road was a dead end, he still started down the north side. *All the older kids park their cars at the end,* he thought, *and I bet they litter the whole place with cans.*

45

Many of the houses were hidden from the road. *Man, I wonder who lives in here? They must really be rich. The only person I've heard about is the Old Bag.*

He filled the second pillowcase and started putting cans into the wagon. Sweat trickled down his forehead.

"Hey, you're picking up all the cans!" Paul looked up, startled. An old woman peered at him from behind the shrubbery. He wanted to turn around and run, but he knew all the cans would fall off the wagon. *It's the Old Bag. All the kids at school say she's crazy.*

"Are you thirsty?" the old woman asked him, a warm smile on her face. "I just made some fresh lemonade."

"I, uh, don't think I want any," Paul blurted out. "And I have to leave now."

"Are you sure?" the woman said. "Or are you just leaving because you don't want to be seen with the Old Bag?"

Paul's face began to turn red. "I don't know."

"Well I do." The woman's face darkened. "Ever since my husband died and I have lived alone, children have teased me. They call me names, tip over my garbage cans, and somebody even threw eggs at my garage."

"I didn't do that," Paul said. "I've never been down here before. I just heard . . . ."

"So you have heard about me, haven't you?" The woman stopped smiling. "I guess you're just like the rest of them. You think just because someone is old that she doesn't have feelings."

"No I don't," Paul answered. "I've decided that I want some lemonade." He pulled the wagon off to the side of the road. "But I can't stay long. I have to collect a lot more cans."

"What for? Are you interested in ecology?" the woman asked, her white hair blowing in the gentle breeze.

"Our school is having an auction to raise money for a refugee family," Paul replied, "and everybody is supposed to bring something tomorrow. Mom and I don't have anything to give so I'm going to sell these cans tonight and give the money. It won't be much, but it's better than showing up without anything. Some of the other guys are bringing dryers and really expensive stuff."

"Now I understand," the woman said. "You do have to hurry and get them before dark. Come on in." She held open the screen door for him. "I heard about the auction on the radio."

"This is a really neat room," Paul said, his eyes wide. "Where'd you get all those beautiful carvings?"

"My husband collected them," the woman said. "We used to travel a lot. He worked for the airlines."

Paul walked over to a shelf of old bottles. "Gee, these sure look old. Where'd you get them?"

"My husband knew a man who ran a bulldozer. One day he was digging a foundation for a house and dug them up."

Paul picked up a silver pocket watch with a horse engraved on the back. "How do you wind this? It doesn't have anything to turn."

The woman laughed. "It has a little key, but I wouldn't use it now. The watch goes way back in my family, and it might break." She poured the lemonade. "Sit down and cool off."

"Thanks."

"I'm Mrs. Penner. What's your name?"

"Paul Fields. I live on Brookside."

Paul soon learned that Mrs. Penner had been one of the first people to build in the city. "My husband built this house himself," she said proudly. "Would you like to see some old photographs?"

"Sure."

She pulled out some old photograph albums, and Paul was fascinated. Then she showed him her collection of canes, the secret panel in the kitchen where she used to hide her silverware when she and her husband were traveling, and even an old musket that had been used during the Civil War.

"Oh," he exclaimed suddenly. "I have to finish getting cans. It'll be dark in two hours, and I'd like to get as many as possible."

"Surely the school isn't forcing you to bring something expensive?" Mrs. Penner asked. "I thought everyone just donated things."

Paul quickly explained. "So you see," he added, "I want to make up for losing the game today, and I don't want to make everyone mad at me."

"But if your class loses, it won't just be your fault, will it?"

"No, but they might think it is, and that's the same thing." Paul stood up. "Thanks for inviting me in. You're sure not an Old Bag."

Mrs. Penner laughed again. "Thanks. I may be old, but I still am interested in lots of things. Come back sometime, will you?"

"OK."

Paul pushed open the door and was nearly to the road when Mrs. Penner called to him. "Wait, Paul, I have something for you." He turned around. "I'd like you to take this to the auction tomorrow." She held up a dirty bottle with a rusty wire cap. "I'll put it in a box for you so it won't be broken. It'll just take a minute."

Paul packed the small box carefully in the wagon. He continued picking up cans until it was too dark to see. After squashing them flat, he took them to the store.

"Here is $5.60," the man said.

"Is that all?" Paul asked. "I had so many cans."

"Yes, you did," the man replied, "but we can only pay you a penny apiece."

When Paul returned home, he found that his mother had already eaten. "Sorry to have to leave again," his mother had written, "but I had to finish up some important work. Hope you found a lot of cans. Go ahead and finish the chicken."

Paul ate quickly and went to bed after putting the wagon away and setting the little box with the bottle in it by his bed.

The next morning, he explained to his mother what had happened and showed her the bottle. "I wonder why she gave that to you?" his mother said. "I guess she wanted to help."

"Yeah, she was trying," Paul said, "and even if it is only a bottle, it still meant a lot to her. She told me that her husband liked it better than any of the others."

"I want to help, too," Paul's mother said. "I have half a day off because I've worked extra hours. I'd like to help the refugee family get settled. Everything will be so new to them."

"Maybe we can help them learn English." Paul was feeling happier than he had in days. "Thanks, Mom. I'll tell my teacher."

When Paul arrived at school and walked into the large gym, several boys walked up to him. "Hi, Paul. What did you bring?"

"Hi, Jared. I brought some money and this." He held up the bottle quickly and then put it back into the box.

"Why it's just a bottle," another boy said.

"Yeah." Tony walked up beside Paul. "We'll probably lose for sure. Look at all the neat things everybody has brought. We don't have a chance to win." He sighed. "And you bring an old bottle."

"Why don't you put your box over here, Paul?" Mr. Adamson said. "Good, you've got your grade on it."

It won't make any difference, Paul thought. *It's just an old bottle.*

Right after lunch, the doors opened and people began looking at the donations. When school was out at two-thirty, the students crowded into the gym.

"They're almost done bidding," Jared said to Paul. "They started at twelve."

"Who's winning?"

"Eighth grade is way ahead," Jared said. "Somebody brought a horse trailer. There are just a few items that haven't been bid on yet."

Paul looked at the table of small items. "They still haven't bid on my bottle."

"I know. It won't matter, though. The eighth graders are too far ahead."

Several minutes later, the auctioneer held up the bottle and began chanting in a singsong voice. Immediately people began bidding.

"They want it!" Paul exclaimed. "They want the bottle."

The prices continued to rise, and the gymnasium grew quiet when one man bid two hundred dollars. Then someone else bid two hundred fifty dollars! Minutes later, the auctioneer said loudly, "Sold to number sixty-four for three hundred dollars."

"We won!" Jared shouted. "Look at the total on the chalkboard. We beat the eighth graders by fifty dollars."

Paul grinned, thinking about Mrs. Penner. *I bet she knew it was worth that much all the time.*

Suddenly Tony towered in front of him. "You know, I'm sorry for saying what I did to you today, Paul. I just didn't think that a dirty bottle would be worth that much. Where'd you get it?"

"A special woman gave it to me," Paul said. "Maybe I'll introduce you to her sometime, but not until we get back from Starved Rock."

LET'S THINK ABOUT IT

Even though some people thought Mrs. Penner was strange because she was old and lived alone, she turned out to be kind and generous when Paul took time to get to know her. Likewise, the bottle everyone thought was worthless turned out to be really valuable. In the Old Testament—1 Samuel 16:1-13— you can read how God sent Samuel to choose a new king for Israel. At first Samuel only looked at people's outward appearances, but in verse 7, God told him to pay more attention to other things.

◆ ◆ ◆

Lord, thank you for loving me the way I am on the inside, even if other people judge me by my outward appearance. To you, what I am becoming inside is what really matters. Help me see the good in other people. Amen.

The Lost Knife

"Hey, Michael, let's go tubing before lunch!"

Michael Stevens looked down at the small pile of wood shavings between his knees and leaned back against the tree. "Sure, I'll go with you." He laid down his knife and the block of wood and put on his old tennis shoes. "I'm not going to hurt my feet on the sharp rocks like I did last time."

"Hurry up," Josh said impatiently. "There are some neat rapids around that bend."

Josh and Michael picked up their inner tubes and started walking. "Boys," Mrs. Stevens said, "be careful not to go past this rock. The water is a lot higher than it was last year, and you're not wearing life jackets or helmets."

"We'll be careful," Michael said. "You tell us that every year."

"I mean it every year," she answered.

"I'm glad you're going in that cold water and not me," Michael's sister, Joan, said. "You wouldn't catch me doing that. I think I'll stand down by this rock and look at your blue skin when you get out of the water."

"We won't get that cold," Josh said. "There isn't a wind, and the air is warm."

A few minutes later, the boys waded into the river and sat down in their tubes. The swift current swept them downstream and tugged at their legs. "It's getting faster," Josh yelled. "Look at the narrow places we'll go through." He clung to the inner tube. "This is fun. It's not as hard as I thought it would be. Maybe that's because our tubes are bigger." Suddenly, in the middle of the third set of rapids, Josh's tube swung into a large rock and flipped over.

"Now watch me," Michael shouted, bobbing past Josh, who was standing in the shallow water. "I bet I can make it." He wedged himself in tightly. Faster and faster he went, narrowly missing the rock that Josh had hit and shooting around the curve.

"Look," Joan shouted from the hill. "He's heading for the deep water!"

Thinking that his sister was cheering him on and unable to understand her words above the roar of the rushing water, Michael waved. He didn't realize that he had already gone down too far. The fast water caught his tube and drove it toward the lower rapids. Frantically trying to hold on, he dodged one large rock but slammed into another.

54

"Try to get over to this rock," his father shouted, running to the edge of the river. "Then I can lift you out."

Michael kicked his feet and paddled furiously. As he saw the water boiling over the rocks below, he gave one last kick and grabbed hold of a slippery rock.

"Hold on," his father shouted. "Don't let go."

I won't if I can help it, Michael thought.

Suddenly the current swung Michael's tube into the fast water again and flipped him over. The tube popped out from under him and, feeling the current suck him under, he lunged for another rock. His fingers found a handhold; he clung to the rock even though his arm felt like it was being pulled out of its socket.

"I've got you," his father yelled. "Let go!" His large hand squeezed Michael's wrist and pulled him up the side of the rock.

"I knew you shouldn't be doing that without wearing life jackets and helmets," his mother said. "Are you all right?"

"I guess so." Michael sprawled on a large, flat rock, feeling the warm sun on his back.

"I wasn't sure I could reach you," his father said, breathing heavily. "When you flipped over, I thought at first that you were still hanging onto the tube."

"It's a good thing I wasn't," Michael answered. "Look, it's being pounded against the rocks."

"Now you've wrecked it for me," Joan said. "Nobody will ever let me go tubing again."

Michael rubbed his bruised ribs. "You've done dumb things, too. How about that time when you got lost because you decided not to stay on the main trail? The park rangers had to go out and find you."

"That's enough," Mr. Stevens said. "Let's just be thankful that neither of you were hurt. We can always buy another tube."

"I can't wait to start eating the fried chicken," Joan said. She walked over to the picnic basket. "Can I have some milk now, Mother?"

Mrs. Stevens nodded. "Sure, but save some for the rest of us."

Josh and Michael walked over to where they had piled their clothes. "That was close," Michael said, putting on his pants over his dripping shorts. "I thought I was going right into the lower rapids."

"I thought I was, too," Josh said, "but that rock stopped me in the shallow water. We should have started up higher."

Michael stopped buttoning his shirt and reached into his pocket. Then he looked down at the ground. "I can't find my knife. Have you seen it?"

"No. Where'd you have it last?"

"I put it in my pants pocket, I think," Michael said slowly. "I know I had it just before we went into the water." He got down on his hands and knees, running his fingers over the ground.

"What are you doing?" Joan asked. "It's time to eat."

"I know," Michael said crossly. "I lost my knife and I have to find it."

"The knife can wait," Joan said. "My stomach can't."

"Joan's right," Mrs. Stevens said. "Come over and eat. You can look for the knife later."

"I can't, Mom. I lost the knife Grandpa gave me for my birthday. It's the one I use for wood carving because the blades are small."

"You've got other knives," Joan said, coming over to where Josh and Michael were crawling around. "What difference does one knife make?"

"A lot of difference to me," Michael snapped. "Have you ever lost something that meant a lot to you?"

"Yeah," Joan replied. "I lost my ring at the beach and never did find it."

"Well, the knife means a lot to me," Michael said, "and I'm going to keep looking for it."

"Would it help if I looked too?" Joan asked.

Mr. Stevens walked over and joined them. "If it's here, we'll find it," he stated. "It can't be far. When did you last have it?"

"I was whittling this piece of wood before we went tubing."

"Joan, you look over there," Mr. Stevens said. "I once lost a pocketknife, and I remember how it felt."

"Did you find it?" Josh asked hopefully.

"No."

As Michael stood up to pull a sticker out of his thumb, he saw a glint of silver in a small hole by the edge of a long tree root. "I see it," he shouted, "but I can't get it out. Somebody must have accidentally kicked it."

"We have a coat hanger in the car that could hook it," Mr. Stevens said. A few minutes later, he bent the end of the hanger into a small hook.

"Be careful, Dad," Michael said. "If it drops off the hanger, it'll go even deeper where we can't see it anymore." He knelt down and watched as his father carefully snagged the ring on the knife and eased it out of the hole.

"We've got it!" Michael said, a grin spreading across his face. "Fried chicken, here we come."

LET'S THINK ABOUT IT

Even though his knife wasn't worth a lot of money, Michael kept looking for it until he found it because it meant a lot to him. As Jesus stood in front of a large group of people, he told his disciples that God cares about every person, just as he cares about something as small as a sparrow. You can read what Jesus said in the New Testament—Luke 12:6, 7.

◆   ◆   ◆

Thank you for loving me the way I am, even though I sometimes feel lost in the crowd and wonder why you remember me. You have created me for a purpose, and you won't forget about me. Thank you, too, for caring about even little things in my life that matter to me. Amen.

The Keewansett Harbor Rescue

Chris Landrum brushed the sand off his feet and pulled open the screen door. "Is it time to eat yet?"

"Just about," Uncle Jim answered, looking up from his newspaper. "How was the beach?"

"Taffy and I had fun," Chris replied, bending down to pat his tan cocker spaniel. "We walked along the shore toward the harbor, and then I looked for starfish. I found several in a small pool, but I left them there because they were still alive."

"You could have kept them to put on our shelf in the living room," Aunt Mary said, putting napkins on the table. "After all, this is the first time you've been here." She pointed to a cupboard. "We have some pretty shells in there, but we haven't gotten them out yet."

"How can you go back to the city after spending the summer here?"

"I enjoy teaching," Aunt Mary answered, "and by the end of the summer I'm ready to go back."

"Chris," Uncle Jim said, "your aunt and I have decided to go sailing after lunch. Do you want to go too?"

"No, I'd rather stay here."

"How come?"

"I don't like the water," Chris said, frowning.

"We'll have life jackets. You'll be OK."

"I'd rather stay here and read." Chris pointed to the bookshelf. "You have some good books."

"If you'd take time to learn how to swim," Aunt Mary said quietly, "you wouldn't be afraid of the water. Then you'd enjoy it a lot more."

"I don't want to learn now," Chris stated.

"OK, but the woman at the public pool said she'd teach you when the pool isn't too crowded." Aunt Mary placed the hamburgers on the table. "Let's eat."

After the prayer, Chris ate quietly, listening to his aunt and uncle discuss the next sailboat they were going to buy. Finally he said, "Look at the dark clouds."

Uncle Jim looked out the kitchen window. "They're all right. It'll take a good while for them to reach us. We'll have plenty of time to get back."

"Still, we'd better get going." Aunt Mary stood up. "Will you do the dishes? We'll bring back some fried clams for dinner." Minutes later, they walked to the shed and took out the life preservers and bailing bucket. Chris waved good-bye as they got into the car.

An hour later, he looked up from his book. "It's getting darker, Taffy," he said, "and the wind is getting a lot stronger." The dog jumped up next to him. "It's a good day for reading."

As Chris neared the end of an exciting chapter, Taffy ran to the door and whined. "You want to go out?" Chris asked, putting down his book. "Even though it's starting to sprinkle?"

Sand made a swishing noise against the side of the cottage and blew into his eyes when he stepped outside. A shutter on a nearby cottage flapped back and forth. *I hope Uncle Jim and Aunt Mary hurry back into the harbor,* he thought. He watched several power-boats return from the ocean while Taffy ran in little circles on the sand.

"OK, Taffy, let's go back in." Taffy walked obediently through the door, and Chris started reading again. Twenty minutes later, Taffy whined again. "I just took you out," Chris said. "You don't have to go out. Besides, it's starting to rain pretty hard now."

Her ears cocked, Taffy scratched on the door.

"OK, OK, I'll let you out." Chris opened the door a crack, and Taffy darted to a clump of beach grass and started barking. "This is no time to play. Come back," Chris said, but the dog wouldn't budge. "Taffy, come back here," he commanded again.

"Stupid dog," he muttered, putting on his gym shoes and a warm sweatshirt. "Now I have to get wet, too." He closed the door tightly and ran after Taffy. Rather than staying in one spot, however, Taffy ran toward the jetty. "Taffy," Chris called harshly, "come back here!"

Suddenly Chris thought he heard a faint voice coming from the ocean. He walked over to the dunes at the edge of the beach, watching the waves breaking in the harbor. *I'm sure Aunt Mary and Uncle Jim are back now.* He looked into the harbor and saw that most of the boats had moored.

When he turned to look at the jetty, he noticed a white sailboat pitching and rolling in the waves. *Even though the wind is blowing into the harbor, they'll never get in against the tide. Waves are already breaking over the bow.*

Chris coaxed Taffy back into the house and opened the shed door before remembering that Uncle Jim had taken the extra life preserver to sit on. He slid down the sand dune, wishing he had brought a raincoat. The wind cut through his sweatshirt as he began climbing the huge rocks on the jetty to get closer to the boat.

The waves on the ocean side of the jetty smashed against the rocks, throwing fountains of spray into the air. Several times he slipped on the rocks. The farther out he climbed, the higher the waves became. To his left, the dark tidal current swept along the jetty toward the ocean. A board bobbed quickly by and then was buried in the boiling water where the outgoing tide and the wind-driven waves met at the end of the jetty. *If I fell in now, with no life jacket on, nobody would ever find me.* He looked at the boat again. *Hey, now they're trying to get back out into the ocean, away from the jetty.*

As the boat drew closer, he tightened his hood to keep out most of the salt spray and moved to the center of the jetty to stay as far away from the water as possible.

The man in the bow of the sailboat was bailing furiously with a plastic bucket while a woman kept trying to sail into the ocean. But the wind pushed the boat back toward the rocks. *If they don't do something soon, they'll be smashed against the jetty,* Chris thought.

Even as he watched, the small boat was swept toward him on the crest of a large wave. "We're trying to go back out," the man shouted, "but we can't do it. The wind is too strong, and the tide keeps us out of the harbor. Call the Coast Guard."

"I can't," Chris called back through cupped hands. "We don't have a phone."

The man shouted something else, but the boiling waves and a gust of wind drowned out his words.

Chris inched his way out farther, stepping carefully so that he wouldn't slip down the side of a rock into the water. The salt water on his lips tasted bitter, and he began shivering.

As he reached the end of the jetty where the water dashed against the rocks with a deafening roar, a large wave swept toward him. He braced himself against a large rock, and then the wave hit. Water cascaded over the rock in front of him and rushed up to his knees. The sailboat spun around wildly. Its boom nearly knocked the woman in the stern out of the boat, which careened broadside toward the jetty and hit the rocks hard. The man tried to keep the boat off the rocks with a wooden paddle, but it broke in half.

"Let's get out," the man shouted. He crouched down until the boat hit the rocks again, and then he half jumped, half fell onto the jetty.

The boat smashed against the rocks a third time and began to sink. Suddenly the woman fell out! *I can't get any closer,* Chris thought. *I could fall in, too.* But as the woman bobbed toward the jetty, Chris scrambled beside a large rock and leaned out over the water. Waves broke in his face as he grabbed hold of the woman's hand. "Help me," Chris screamed at the man who was climbing toward him. "She's pulling me in, too."

The man slid down beside Chris and together they pulled the woman up the side of the jetty. A gaping hole in its side, the boat tipped over and sank.

Fighting back tears of exhaustion and fear, wondering if his aunt and uncle had returned safely to the harbor, Chris helped the couple cross the rocks. His knee and shoulder hurt from being banged against a rock, and the man's arm was bleeding.

Rock by rock, they struggled back to the cottage. "Here are some towels," Chris said, "and some blankets. I'll get the first-aid kit from the bathroom and some clothes for you."

His clothes dripping onto the wooden floor, Chris lit a fire in the fireplace and put tea on while the man and woman changed clothes. Only then did he put on dry clothes himself.

"What were you doing out there?" the man asked Chris as he drank the tea.

"My dog started whining. I thought at first that you were my aunt and uncle coming back. Your boat looked like theirs."

"It doesn't look like much now," the man said sadly.

"You mean, they're still out there?" the man's wife asked.

"I hope not." Chris said, swallowing hard. "They've been gone a long time. It's only a ten-minute ride to the docks."

"I'm sorry."

Chris sat down in front of the fire, too, and then stood up when someone knocked at the door.

"Are you Chris?" a girl asked as soon as he opened the door.

"Yes."

"Your aunt called us a few minutes ago. When the squall hit, they beached their boat a mile down, near the public beach. They tried to get into the harbor twice before it got too rough, but the outgoing tide was already too strong." The girl looked at the couple by the fire and noticed the man's bloodstained bandage. "What happened?"

As they told their story, Taffy whined again. "Oh no you don't," Chris whispered, trying to hold back a sneeze. "I'm not going out there again." Then he added, "But I am going to sign up for swimming lessons."

LET'S THINK ABOUT IT

Although Chris was afraid of the water, he still went out onto the jetty to help the man and the woman. In the New Testament—Matthew 8:23-27—you can read how Jesus' disciples became terribly afraid as they crossed a stormy lake in a boat. Rather than having faith in Jesus, they woke him up so that he'd keep them from drowning.

◆　　◆　　◆

Thank you, Lord, for giving me courage to do things that are hard for me. Please help me always to remember that you are with me. Help me have faith that you will work things out for the best even when nothing seems to be going right. Amen.

"Will They Like Me?"

As the bell rang, Mrs. Puckett turned from the chalkboard. A thin boy stood inside the door. "Hello," she said, smiling. "What can I do for you?"

"This is my first day," the boy said, "and the principal sent me here."

"What's your name?"

"Rawlins Leekey," the boy replied, and several girls in the class giggled.

"Well, Rawlins, why don't you take that seat in the second row?" She pointed. "I'm Mrs. Puckett. We're working on adjectives today."

Rawlins sat down and looked around. Several boys were sitting sideways in their chairs and staring at him.

A redhaired girl in front of him leaned across the aisle and whispered something to a plump girl with glasses.

I wonder if they'll like me? he thought. He frowned and tried to concentrate on what Mrs. Puckett was saying.

Finally the bell rang. "Class is dismissed," Mrs. Puckett said. "Rawlins, could you come up here for just a minute?"

Chairs scraped across the tile floor, voices rose, and soon only Rawlins and his teacher were left. "Did I do something wrong?" he asked.

"Oh, no," Mrs. Puckett said, chuckling. "I just want to make sure that you know your schedule for the rest of the day."

Rawlins shifted his weight from one foot to the other and held out a piece of paper. "The principal gave me a schedule. I go to lunch now."

"That's right." Mrs. Puckett looked over the list and handed it back. "You're all set, then. The cafeteria is downstairs and to the left. You'll hear all the noise. After lunch, your math class is in room 100. It's on the same floor."

"Thanks." Rawlins walked downstairs and got in the cafeteria line.

"Hey, Rawlins!" A tall boy near the cash register turned around. "Where'd you get a name like Rawlins Leekey?" Rawlins shrugged his shoulders and didn't say anything. The boy laughed, and several other boys glanced at Rawlins.

Rawlins felt his face turning red. He wished he could think of something clever to say.

"Excuse me, but you'll need to take a tray." The woman in the white uniform behind the serving counter held up a spoonful of green beans. Rawlins reached back, pulled a tray off the stack, and slid it along the rail. He felt drops of sweat running down his neck and paid for the food at the cash register. Then he walked into the cafeteria and began looking for a place to sit down.

"Hey, Rawlins, you can sit with us. We're really pretty harmless," the boy continued, "and you're so skinny you won't take up much room."

Feeling uncomfortable, Rawlins walked past the crowded tables and sat down by himself. *I wonder what's eating him?* He looked out the window and tried to ignore the noise. *I hope things get better than this.* He thought about the friends he had left in Illinois—Sean whom he'd known since second grade. And the guys in Scouts. Suddenly he realized that someone was talking to him. "I'm sorry," he said, looking up. "I didn't notice you standing there."

"That's okay." The muscular boy brushed the hair off his forehead and smiled. "I saw you standing in the food line and wondered if you're new. I hadn't seen you before."

"I'm Rawlins. This is my first day. We moved here from Illinois."

"I heard Joel Potter giving you a hard time. Don't mind him. He's always putting somebody down. I guess he thinks that he's better than everyone else because he is so tall."

Rawlins forced a smile. "He sure isn't friendly."

71

"No. Just ignore him. Most of the guys are pretty good, but Joel and his friends get their fun at the expense of others. Hey, was your dad transferred?"

"My father decided to sell our farm and come to work for the Patrick Dairy." Rawlins took a bite of potato. "We moved in last Friday."

"I moved here from Texas in February."

"Hey, Ryan." Several boys walked up, and one of them leaned on the table. "Want to shoot baskets with us after school?"

"Sure." Ryan looked toward Rawlins. "This guy just moved here from Illinois. His name's Rawlins."

"Hi," the dark-haired boy replied. "I'm Stephen, and this is Ron. The one with the long nose is Jim."

"You're one to talk," Jim said, grinning.

"Nice to meet you." Rawlins moved his tray over. "Want to sit down? There's plenty of room."

"No thanks. We've got to find enough guys to play." Stephen scanned the rows of tables. "Do you play, Rawlins?"

"A little. I was a forward at my last school."

"We could use another guy. We have lots of fun. And," Stephen said with a smile, "we do win sometimes."

"Where will I meet you? I'll have to run home and get my gym clothes."

"We'll wait for you in the locker room. If we're not there, we'll be in the gym."

"I'll see you later," Rawlins said. He turned to look at two girls who sat down at the other end of the table. *Maybe this school won't be so bad after all.*

LET'S THINK ABOUT IT

When Ryan made an effort to meet Rawlins, he was sensitive to Rawlins' need to feel accepted. While passing through the city of Jericho, Jesus went out of His way to meet Zacchaeus. You can read in the New Testament what Jesus did for Zacchaeus, a tax collector who the people of the city hated because he was suspected of cheating them—Luke 19:1-10.

◆　　◆　　◆

Why do some people always pick on other people, Lord? It hurts me when people make fun of others and try to make themselves look better. When I meet someone who needs a friend, remind me of your love and help me reach out to that person. The more I become a friend, the more friends I will have. Amen.

I'm the Greatest

Peter kicked a rock down the edge of the curb. "I'm glad we won the game against Phil's team. He has a fat head."

"I know. Did you see the look on his face when he threw that long bomb way over Riley's head? I thought he was going to cry." Daniel ran over to a nearby tree and started swinging on a branch.

"I didn't think we were going to win until Toby threw that pass to me on the ten-yard line." Peter grinned. "I wasn't even sure I was going to catch it. I had to stoop down."

"What about the time I ran around the left side and got to the twenty-yard line? That gave us a first down and then you caught another pass." Daniel let go of the branch.

"That was pretty good," Peter agreed, "but it was my catch that got us right up to the goal line so we could get the last touchdown."

Daniel didn't say anything as he walked over to the curb. "Are you saying," he finally said, sitting down, "that if it weren't for your catch our team would have lost?"

Peter looked down at him. "If you put it that way, yes. My catch got us close to the goal line."

"I don't think it was all that great a catch," Daniel stated. "You should have gotten a touchdown with it, and you didn't. Besides, you nearly dropped it."

"So what? I caught it, didn't I?" Peter's heart began beating faster.

"If it weren't for my run, you never would have gotten that close."

"Is that so? You sound just like Phil now." Peter danced around in a circle, waving his arms and shouting, "Look at me, look at me."

"Cut that out! What do you mean *I* sound like Phil? You're the one who said that if it weren't for your catch we'd have lost." Daniel stood up. "You know, the things you do surprise me sometimes." He leaned down and picked up his books.

"It isn't all my fault." Peter stepped back. "You're the one who started it by saying that your run was the best." His voice grew louder.

Daniel looked at his friend. "You know, I never meant to say that my run was the greatest move in the game. If you really think that your catch was the best, that's all right with me. I don't really care."

Peter relaxed and leaned against a tree. "I don't feel that way. It doesn't matter to me, either. We worked together as a team and had fun playing a good game." He took a deep breath. "How'd we even get into this?"

"We were talking about Phil blowing that pass."

"Yeah, and now we're starting to sound like him." Peter walked over to Daniel. "Why don't we forget about who was the greatest and stay friends?"

"Sounds good to me." Daniel picked up his jacket, and the two boys continued walking down the street.

LET'S THINK ABOUT IT

As the disciples walked with Jesus to the city of Capernaum, they started arguing over who was the greatest. Read what Jesus taught them about greatness in the New Testament—Mark 9:33-35.

◆   ◆   ◆

I like people to realize the good things I do, Lord, and when they ignore me I get angry. Help me realize that because of your love for me, I don't have to be perfect and prove that I'm better than everybody else. I can be the greatest because you created me the way I am. Amen.

A Wrong Decision

Gary Wilson walked slowly down the road, carrying several scrap two-by-fours. He kicked a pop can off the road's edge, and it clattered down the rocky slope. *I wonder if the house is vacant?* he thought, looking at a stone house built against the side of a cliff. The lower windows had iron bars across them, and the shades were drawn. Weeds were everywhere, and bits of newspaper lay on the porch and underneath the evergreen trees. He walked to the side of the house. *What's in this shed?* After rattling the padlock on the door, he looked in the window and saw a hammer hanging on a nail. *It won't hurt to go inside. Nobody's around anyway.*

He laid the wood down and pushed up on the window frame as hard as he could. A nail caught and bent as the window went up. While he was crawling inside, a car drove down the hill. He grabbed hold of a table and pulled, but his feet were still hanging out when the car passed.

Covered with dust, Gary was finally able to stand up. Tools were piled on a long shelf, and several buckets held odd-sized bolts and nails. *There's a lot of stuff here,* he thought, picking up a chisel and a screwdriver. *Nobody will miss these tools. There are so many.* He dropped the tools out the window and began squirming out. As he dropped to the ground, his pants caught on the nail and ripped. *Just my luck,* he thought, looking down at his pants. *How will I explain that to Mom?* He closed the window, picked up the tools and lumber, and started walking.

"Just a minute. You've gone far enough." The man's voice was deep. "Don't run. Just turn around."

Gary turned around slowly. "What's wrong?"

"Well," the tall man said, walking closer, "around here we notice when strangers come around. When I saw you poking around this house," he motioned, "I decided to see what you were up to."

"I was just looking to see if anyone lived there." Gary tried to hide the tools beneath the two-by-fours.

"The Andersons are in Arizona, and I keep an eye on their house." The man walked closer. "What's your name?"

"Gary Wilson." Gary took a step backward and started to run.

"Oh no you don't!" The man lunged and grabbed Gary's shirt. "You've got some explaining to do first. What's in your hand?"

80

"Just some wood and some tools." Gary held them out. "The tools are pretty old."

"Yes, they are. Give them to me." After looking them over, the man continued, "Where did you get these?"

"I found them."

"What are you doing up here?"

"My grandpa lives down the road, and we're visiting him."

The man tightened his grip. "I think it's time you and I went to see him." Gary walked in front, with the man following closely. "I'd stay put if I were you," the man cautioned. "Just keep walking and don't get any strange notions." They walked until the road forked. "Which way?" the man asked.

"Left," Gary mumbled.

"Is Sam Hopkins your grandpa?"

"Yeah."

"He's a friend of mine," the man stated. "He won't like what you did, will he?"

"I don't know what you mean."

"All right, be that way. You're only getting yourself in deeper." The man pointed up the driveway. "Let's go."

Gary pushed open the screen door.

"Where have you been, Gary?" his mother asked. "Oh my, look at your pants. What did you do?" Before Gary could answer, his mother noticed the man standing outside. "Oh, I didn't see you. I'm Gary's mother."

"I figured that."

"Is something wrong?" Mrs. Wilson asked.

"I'm afraid there is, Ma'am," the man replied. "I'm Bill Muren, and I live down the road a ways. May I come in?"

"Of course."

At that moment, a white-haired man entered the hallway. "Why, hello, Bill! Come on in. What brings you here this morning? Shouldn't you be building that fence?"

"Yes, Sam, but some things have to be settled first." Bill looked at Gary. "I caught this boy stealing some tools out of the Andersons' shed." He laid the chisel and screwdriver on the kitchen table. "He got that rip in his pants as he climbed out the window."

"Is that true, Gary?" Mrs. Wilson stared at her son.

"Yeah," Gary answered, "but I wasn't going to keep them."

"What were you going to do with them?" she asked. When Gary didn't reply, she continued, "Will you please explain exactly what happened, Mr. Muren?"

When he finished telling what he had seen, Mrs. Wilson sighed. "I'm disappointed in you, Gary." She walked over to the fireplace and turned to Bill. "Thank you for bringing this to my attention. I'll handle things now, unless he broke something getting into the shed."

"No, he didn't do that," Bill said quietly. "I'm sorry this happened and that I had to be the one to catch your son. But," he added, "we can't have this kind of thing going on up here." He exchanged looks with Gary's grandfather. "I'll stop by on Saturday, Sam."

When the door closed, Mrs. Wilson sat down at the table. "Gary, what you did deserves strong punishment. You know that. Not only did you try to steal the tools, you made Grandpa look bad in front of his friend." She paused. "I'm going to call your father and tell him that we are both coming home."

"But, Mom, we just got here, and you promised that I could stay here for a week." Gary jumped up. "Why can't you leave me here and punish me later?"

Mrs. Wilson's lip trembled. "There's nothing more to be said. I know how much you were looking forward to staying here. But now that you've done this, the plans have changed. I'm sure your father will have more to say about it when you get home."

LET'S THINK ABOUT IT

Often the temptation to do something wrong comes when we least expect it, but we can still choose not to give in. When Gary, for example, felt the desire to break into the shed, he could have chosen to walk the other way, but he didn't. When Satan tempted Jesus in the wilderness, Jesus refused to give in. You can read in the New Testament what Jesus said to Satan—Matthew 4:1-11.

◆   ◆   ◆

It's hard to live the type of life you want me to live, Lord. Sometimes it seems that everywhere I go I am tempted to do something wrong. Give me the strength to resist temptation and to know when to ask you for help. Thank you that temptation itself isn't wrong and help me realize that I'm committing sin only when I give in to temptation. Amen.

Butch Runs Away

Mrs. Stewart opened the door a crack to let the terrier out. "Stay in the yard, Butch," she said. Then she watched through the window as the dog started lapping at the snow.

Mr. Stewart called to his wife. "How about helping me build a fire? We can make popcorn and play Scrabble. No sense going out this afternoon unless we have to. We have all the presents, and the roads should be cleared by tomorrow so we can get to church."

After the two of them laid the kindling on the hearth, their son, Andy, ran upstairs from the basement. "Can I light it?"

"I don't see why not," his father answered. "Let me put some logs on first."

Soon the living room was filled with warmth and the aroma of popcorn. "Where's Butch?" Andy asked suddenly. "I want him to get this piece of popcorn I dropped."

"Oh, no." His mother rushed from the table and pressed her face against the kitchen window. "I let him out nearly an hour ago, and I forgot about him."

"He'll freeze!" Andy exclaimed. He put on his boots and jacket. "I'll go get him." At that moment, a gust of wind rattled the window.

"I still don't see him," his mother said, "but he can't have gone far. With the snow blowing so much, he could be right by the porch and we still couldn't see him."

"I'll find him," Andy said confidently.

"Don't be gone too long," his mother cautioned.

Andy stepped into a snowdrift and walked around the house to the street. The wind blew snow into his face and down his neck, and he wished he had worn a scarf. The heavy snow nearly covered his boots. "Butch, come here, boy," he called. "Come on."

After going up and down the block for nearly ten minutes, Andy decided to look in the neighbors' backyards. He trudged through the drifts, once sinking up to his knees, but he couldn't see any tracks.

"What are you doing?" a woman called out from her back door.

"I'm looking for my dog, Butch. He's a terrier. Have you seen him?"

"No, I haven't," the woman said. "Isn't it too cold to look for a dog?"

"Oh, no," Andy stated. "I want him home when we open our presents tonight. He always tears up the wrapping paper."

The woman smiled. "Hope you find him. Merry Christmas."

Rubbing his gloves together, Andy walked through all the backyards and turned down another street. "Butch, Butch," he repeated as the wind blew between the houses. "Where are you?"

A garage door opened, and a man carrying a snow shovel walked out. "Hi," he said. "It sure is nice to get snow on Christmas Eve, isn't it?"

"Yes," Andy said, "but I can't find my dog. Have you seen him?"

"What color is he?" the man asked, walking closer.

"He's brown." Andy pulled his cap down over his ears. "Mom let him out, and now I can't find him. We just moved here, and he doesn't know his way around."

"I'm sure he'll come home," the man said. "Do you want some hot cider before you start looking again? My wife just made some."

"No, I want to find Butch before my sister gets home. She went to a friend's house."

"OK," the man said, "but be careful. With this wind, it's a lot colder than you think."

"I'll be all right," Andy said. "I'm used to being outside."

He walked to the next corner and turned left. His footprints quickly filled with snow. When he saw a snowplow coming toward him, Andy had an idea.

He ran toward it, staying to the side of the road, and waved his hands for the driver to stop. The snow spinning off the plow slowed down and the driver stopped. A serious look on his face, the bearded man rolled down his window. "What's wrong?" he asked.

"Have you seen a brown terrier?" Andy asked. "He ran away, and he doesn't know his way home. We just moved here."

"No, but I'll keep a sharp lookout." The man studied Andy carefully. His cheeks were bright red. "Hop in," he said cheerfully. "I need to take a break anyway, and you can get warm."

"I can't," Andy replied. "I have to find my dog. My parents have a fire going and everything."

"I can understand that," the man stated. "My wife cooked a turkey, and I can't wait to eat it. I have a daughter about your age," he added, "and I'm giving her a new bicycle."

"Will you tell her about Jesus being born in a manger?" Andy asked. "My parents read that to us every Christmas Eve."

The man thought for a moment. "We haven't done that in years, but it might be a good idea." He put his jacketed arm out the window. "Yeah, it is a good idea. It's easy to forget the real meaning of Christmas." He motioned. "Like this snow. It's so beautiful, and even if it means I have to work all day today, I still like it."

"I do too," Andy said, "but it makes it harder to find my dog."

"Are you sure you don't want to get warm?" the man asked again.

"No, thanks. He can't have gone too far." Andy started walking, and with a roar the snowplow began to move. He turned and watched as the truck began spitting cinders out the back.

Andy turned down a street lined with evergreens and brushed some snow off the side of a car. At the end of the block, he noticed several kids making a snowman. "Hi," he said, walking up to them. "Have you seen my dog?"

"We saw a big collie run by awhile ago," one girl said. "Is he yours?"

"No." Andy's voice dropped. "Butch is just a little terrier."

"What will we do if we see him? We could bring him to your house. Where do you live?"

"I live . . . ," Andy started to say, and then he paused. "I live back there a ways. We just moved here."

"What's the name of the street?"

"I can't remember."

"Well, I guess we aren't much help," the older girl in a red jacket said. "Would you like to help us put the head on the snowman?"

"Sure." Andy and the two girls all lifted together and balanced the head on top. "Sure is a neat snow-man," he said.

"Stay and help us build another one," the older girl said. "I'll go in and get a carrot for the nose."

"I have to get home," Andy said, "but thanks anyway." He turned around and headed down the street again, unable to see his tracks. The snow stung his face now, and his cheeks began to hurt.

"Butch, where are you?" he called out, but his voice was lost in the wind. He kept walking and calling until he became hoarse, and then he stopped at a corner. *Do I go left or right?* The street sign was covered with a sheet of wet snow, and he had to walk around to the other side to read it. "Briar Lane," he said aloud. "I've never heard of that street." A few seconds later, he turned left.

The farther he walked, the less familiar everything looked. A pickup truck he didn't remember seeing was parked in a driveway, and there were no more tire tracks. He trudged farther, still calling, but the familiar bark never answered.

I'm lost, he realized. Then he stopped and tried to remember what a lost person should do. *Don't panic, try to remember where I've walked, and find help.* He looked around and spotted a house with a wreath on the door. *Maybe I shouldn't go up to a house where I don't know the people. Maybe it isn't safe.* In the end, however, he decided to knock on the door.

"Hello," an elderly woman said. "My, my, you're soaked. What are you doing out there?"

"My dog ran away, and I'm trying to find him."

"You're looking in this weather? Come in for a minute and warm up."

Her husband looked up from his puzzle. "If it keeps snowing like this, we may be snowed in all day tomorrow."

"I do have to find my dog," Andy said, removing his gloves and jacket. "We got him when he was just a puppy, and it's Christmas Eve. He's part of the family."

"I know what you mean." The man handed him a cup of hot chocolate. "I lost a colt once when she got out through a broken fence. I had to look for that colt for nearly four hours, and you know where I found her? In the barn. She had more sense than I did. I came huffing and puffing through the deep snow, hardly able to feel my fingers, and there she was, eating hay."

Andy's eyes grew sad. "I've been looking for a long time, but nobody has seen Butch."

"Would it help if I looked, too?" the man asked. "I need some exercise anyway, and this would be as good a time as any to get it."

"OK." Andy waited while the man dressed warmly, and the two of them headed out into the cold.

"Butch," Andy called out from force of habit when they reached the street. "Here, boy."

"Is that him?" the man asked. A small dog was bounding through a snowdrift.

"Butch!" Andy ran toward the dog. "Where have you been?" The dog wagged its tail and licked Andy's face. "I'm sure glad to see you."

"Now we have to get you both home." The man headed back up his driveway. "I'd better drive you. It's starting to get dark." As they got into the car, he asked, "Where do you live?"

"I live in a white house, but I can't remember the street name." Andy looked at the man. "It's in the middle of the block." He hugged Butch as the man backed the car.

They drove for quite a while, up one street and down another, but Andy couldn't recognize his house. "I'm sorry," he finally said. "I just can't remember."

"Let's go back to my home and call your parents," the man said.

"The phone isn't connected," Andy answered. "They couldn't do it until next week." He looked out the window. "I think I recognize that house, but I'm not sure. Why don't you let Butch and me out here?"

"All right. I'll wait here for a few minutes." The man stopped the car and let them out.

"Thank you," Andy said. "At least I have my dog back."

The man turned the engine off and watched as the boy and his dog walked down the street. *He sure loves that dog.*

When Andy reached the next corner, he turned left but Butch went right. "Come here," he commanded. "Haven't you run around enough today?" He called Butch again, but Butch only ran farther away and whined.

"OK, I'll go that way." Andy followed Butch down the street. Suddenly the dog began running. He ran down the last part of the block and darted across the street.

"Come back here!" Andy ran after him, trying to keep his footing.

When he turned the corner, Butch stood in a driveway, barking. "You did it, Butch," Andy exclaimed. "You brought us home."

He ran up to the door and opened it. "I found him," he called out.

"Great!" Mrs. Stewart hurried into the hallway. "Where was he? You've been gone nearly two hours. I was about ready to contact the police."

Butch walked inside and started shaking himself. Snow and water flew everywhere.

"What a mess," Mrs. Stewart said, and smiled as she patted Butch's head. "But even if you do make a mess, Butch, it's good to have you home. Now we can celebrate Christmas Eve as a family."

While Andy told what had happened, the elderly man drove by, smiling. *I thought that dog would lead him home. Sometimes animals are a bit smarter than people.* He looked at the Christmas lights in the windows and began to hum "Silent Night."

LET'S THINK ABOUT IT

Even though he was cold and lost, Andy refused to stop looking for Butch until he found him. In the New Testament, Jesus tells two parables about a shepherd who looks for a lost sheep and a woman who searches for a lost coin—Luke 15:3-10.

◆　◆　◆

Before I came to you, Lord, my life didn't have real meaning. In many ways, I was lost, too. But then you helped me realize how much I need you and that Jesus died on the cross so that my life could have meaning. Thank you for finding me and for watching over me in every area of my life. Amen.

Dale Breaks a Promise

"Hey, Dale, let's look in that house they're building on Seventh Street." Bob ran up alongside Dale. "My brother told me last night that it will be heated by the sun."

"I can't, Bob," Dale said, continuing to walk. "I always have to go home and change clothes first. Mom wants to know where I go."

"Being late one time won't matter, will it?" Bob stopped at the corner. "Besides, you deserve a break. That math test sure wasn't easy."

"You can say that again." Dale sat down at the edge of the sidewalk and took off his backpack.

"If we're going to the house, we'd better get going," Bob said. "That way, you can get home in a little while and not get into trouble." Bob and Dale cut

across the vacant lot and walked up to the side of the new house.

"How come the builder isn't working here today?" Dale asked, stepping through the doorway.

"I don't know, but it sure makes it easy to look around." The boys laid their jackets and backpacks on the plywood floor and walked quickly through the rooms on the first floor.

"What's this room for?" Dale asked. "It's too small to be a bedroom."

"Maybe it's for the washing machine." Bob dropped a scrap of wood into the basement, and Dale heard a splash. "I'm going up the ladder. Want to come?"

"In a minute. I want to look down here a little longer." Dale examined the pipes in the bathroom and then started up the ladder. After carefully looking into all the upstairs rooms, they walked out onto the balcony. "Hey, Bob, who is the man getting out of that car?"

"I don't know," Bob said. "We'd better get out of here."

"Which way should we go? The back way is all boarded up."

The boys hurriedly started climbing down the rungs. Halfway down, they were startled by the man's voice. "What are you doing here?"

"We were just looking," Dale said. "Bob's brother told him this house was going to be heated by the sun, and we wanted to see what it looked like."

"Do you live around here?"

"I live eight blocks away, and he lives closer."

"What are your names?"

"I'm Dale Carver, and he's Bob Fritz."

"I'm Mr. Spencer, and I'm glad to meet you. This is my house, and I helped design it. There aren't many houses like it in this part of the state." Mr. Spencer walked into a room with large windows. "These insulated windows are designed to catch the sun's rays in the winter, and the roof's overhang will keep out much of the sun in the summer. The floor you're standing on will be covered by thick tiles to hold the heat in the evening. The ceiling," he said, pointing, "has twelve inches of insulation in it."

"What happens if it's cloudy all day in the winter?" Bob asked.

"I'm putting in a wood-burning stove, too, just in case. If you have time, I'll show you around. I'm just checking to see how the work is coming."

The boys followed Mr. Spencer through the house, listening carefully to his enthusiastic explanation. As he was telling them about the skylights, Dale suddenly interrupted. "Bob, what time is it?"

"A little before five o'clock."

"Oh no! I've got to go!" Dale exclaimed. "Thanks for showing me around, Mr. Spencer."

"I'd better go, too," Bob said.

"Come visit me again after we move in," Mr. Spencer said. "I'd prefer that you and your friends not come in here in the meantime. You might get hurt or accidentally break something."

"OK," Bob said. "I'll tell my brother too."

After the boys split up, Dale ran across the vacant lot and took every shortcut he knew. Minutes later, he opened the door. "Hi, Mom, I'm home."

"Where have you been?" His mother turned off the mixer. "I've been expecting you for more than an hour."

"Is it that late already? Bob came up to me while I was coming home and wanted me to do something with him."

"You know that you're supposed to come straight home after school."

"Yeah, but Bob and I got to see that neat house on Seventh Street. Mr. Spencer, the owner, gave us a tour. He says it will have passive solar heat."

"Well, I'm going to have to keep you home from your bicycle trip tomorrow," Mrs. Carver said quietly. "You know the rules."

"But, Mom, I promised the guys I'd show them where the old cemetery is. They are counting on me. And," he continued, "I would have left the house earlier if the man hadn't offered to give us a tour and explain everything."

"It's your own fault," Mrs. Carver said. "The cemetery will still be there next Saturday."

LET'S THINK ABOUT IT

When a man in the Bible named Aaron did not act responsibly, he made excuses rather than admitting his mistake. Like Dale, Aaron didn't stop to think how his actions would affect other people and himself. The story of Aaron's mistake is found in the Old Testament—Exodus 32:1-29.

◆　　◆　　◆

Lord, help me keep my promises and do a good job in whatever I do. Even though it's easy for me to make excuses, change my attitude so that I'll realize how much people count on me. When I prove that I can be trusted, people will give me more responsibility. Amen.